D1568393

WITHDRAWN

LONDON
PUBLIC LIBRARY

LONDON PUBLIC LIBRARY

CHANGING CULTURAL LANDSCAPES

How are people and their communities
affected by migration and settlement?

By Marina Cohen

Crabtree Publishing Company

www.crabtreebooks.com

Author: Marina Cohen
Project director: Ruth Owen
Designer: Elaine Wilkinson
Editors: Mark Sachner, Lynn Peppas
Editorial director: Kathy Middleton
Prepress technician: Katherine Berti
Production coordinator: Margaret Amy Salter
Consultant: Ceri Oeppen BSc, MSc, of the Sussex
    Centre for Migration Research

Developed & Created for Crabtree Publishing Company
by Ruby Tuesday Books Ltd

Front cover (top): Fan dancers take part in a Chinese New Year parade in London.

Front cover (bottom left): A painting by artist Robert Lindneux depicting the suffering of the Cherokee people during The Trail of Tears.

Front cover (bottom center): Bollywood movies from India are now popular worldwide. Here, artists paint a Bollywood poster in London, UK.

Front cover (bottom right): A McDonald's restaurant in Tokyo, Japan

Back cover and title page: Elaborate costumes are an important part of the festival parade during Caribana in Toronto, Canada.

Photo credits:
Alamy: PhotosIndia: pages 3 (left), 28 (top left); Janine Wiedel: page 4 (bottom); ADB Travel: page 7; Bo Zaunders: page 9 (top); page 17 (top); Steffen Hauser: page 18 (bottom); Steve Hamblin: page 23; PeerPoint: page 24; Alan Balmer: page 25; dbtravel: page 28 (center left); Allstar: page 32 (top left); Sven Hoogerhuis: pages 32 (center left), 32 (bottom left); David Grossman: pages 33 (bottom left), 34 (top left), 34 (top right), 36
Corbis: Stephen Hird: front cover (bottom center); Layne Kennedy: pages 8–9 (center); David Paul Morris: page 13; Viviane Moos: pages 26 (bottom), 27; Owen Franken: pages 28 (bottom), 34 (bottom left); Erik Voake: pages 35, 38 (bottom); Ian Hodgson: page 39
Getty Images: Patrick Riviere: pages 19, 22, 29, 42 (left center)
The Granger Collection: pages 10, 11, 17 (bottom), 21 (top)
Library of Congress: pages 14 (bottom), 15, 16 (top), 16 (bottom)
Rex Features: page 31
Ruby Tuesday Books Ltd: page 38
Shutterstock: front cover (top), back cover, pages 1, 3 (center left), 3 (center right), 3 (right), 4 (left), 5 (top), 6, 12 (top), 14 (left), 20 (all), 21 (bottom), 28 (bottom left), 30, 32 (center), 33 (top left), 33 (top right), 33 (bottom right), 33 (right), 34 (bottom right), 34 (bottom x 3), 37 (bottom all), 40–41 (all), 42 (top), 42 (left bottom), 43
Superstock: front cover (bottom left); front cover (bottom right), pages 5 (bottom right), 18 (top)
Wikipedia (public domain): pages 8, 12 (bottom), 26 (top), 37 (top)

Library and Archives Canada Cataloguing in Publication

Cohen, Marina
    Changing cultural landscapes : how are people and their communities affected by migration and settlement? / Marina Cohen.

(Investigating human migration & settlement)
Includes index.
ISBN 978-0-7787-5178-6 (bound).--ISBN 978-0-7787-5193-9 (pbk.)

1. Emigration and immigration--Social aspects--Juvenile literature.
2. Social change--Juvenile literature. 3. Cultural relations--Juvenile literature.
4. Acculturation--Juvenile literature. 5. Assimilation (Sociology)--Juvenile literature. I. Title. II. Series: Investigating human migration & settlement

JV6225.C63 2010   j303.48'2   C2009-905124-9

Library of Congress Cataloging-in-Publication Data

Cohen, Marina.
 Changing cultural landscapes : how are people and their communities affected by migration and settlement? / by Marina Cohen.
    p. cm. -- (Investigating human migration & settlement)
 Includes index.
 ISBN 978-0-7787-5193-9 (pbk. : alk. paper) -- ISBN 978-0-7787-5178-6 (reinforced library binding : alk. paper)
 1. Social change. 2. Cultural relations. 3. Assimilation (Sociology) 4. Acculturation. 5. Emigration and immigration. 6. Land settlement.
 I. Title.
 HM831.C55 2010
 307.209--dc22
                                                    2009034649

Crabtree Publishing Company

Printed in China/122009/CT20090915

www.crabtreebooks.com   1-800-387-7650

Copyright © **2010 CRABTREE PUBLISHING COMPANY**. All rights reserved. No part of this publication may be reproduced, stored in a retrieval system or be transmitted in any form or by any means, electronic, mechanical, photocopying, recording, or otherwise, without the prior written permission of Crabtree Publishing Company. In Canada: We acknowledge the financial support of the Government of Canada through the Book Publishing Industry Development Program (BPIDP) for our publishing activities.

Published in Canada
Crabtree Publishing
616 Welland Ave.
St. Catharines, ON
L2M 5V6

Published in the United States
Crabtree Publishing
PMB 59051
350 Fifth Avenue, 59th Floor
New York, New York 10118

Published in the United Kingdom
Crabtree Publishing
Maritime House
Basin Road North, Hove
BN41 1WR

Published in Australia
Crabtree Publishing
386 Mt. Alexander Rd.
Ascot Vale (Melbourne)
VIC 3032

CONTENTS

CHAPTER ONE

CULTURE AND IDENTITY

People migrate to new areas every day, in just about every part of the world. Any migration of people to a new place is bound to have an impact on everyone concerned, whether they are people already living in that place or members of the migrating group. One impact is the mixing and changing of cultures that occurs when large numbers of people migrate.

What Is Culture?

A group's culture can be expressed in many ways. It might be in the way members of a group behave or in the attitudes, values, or beliefs that people share. Culture also expresses itself in the way members of a group communicate, whether through language and physical gestures or through music, dance, and art. Culture is also embedded in the patterns of a group's everyday life—what members of the group eat, how they dress,

▲◄ Today, the area around Brick Lane in East London is nicknamed "Banglatown" in reference to the area's large immigrant population from Bangladesh. There is a mosque, a Bengali Arts Centre, and a lively market that sells, among other things, sari silks and a huge selection of South Asian foods.

Just 40 years ago many British people had never tasted curry. Today, "going for a curry" has become an important part of leisure culture in the UK.

and the traditions and celebrations in which they participate. All of these characteristics of a group's culture help unite members of the group, giving them a sense of a common identity.

A Strong Sense of Culture

In the 1950s and 1960s, there was a mass migration of Bengalis into the United Kingdom from Bengal, a region that is now divided between India and Bangladesh. A large Bengali community grew in London's East End, and the immigrants retained many aspects of their home culture.

The Mixing of Cultures

The Bengali immigrants had a strong influence on British culture. Some of them had worked as ship's cooks on the long voyages from South Asia to the United Kingdom. Upon settling in their new home, many decided to set up restaurants serving Bengali food.

Today, what is known simply as "Indian food" is among the UK's most popular foods, and many British people consider "curry" to be the UK's new national dish!

FOCUS ON:

FOOD AND CULTURE

Food is an important way in which cultures mix and learn more about each other. Take a walk along some streets in major cities, and you will be able to sample recipes from India, Mexico, Bangladesh, China, Thailand, Korea, Jamaica, Italy—the list goes on! Many immigrants have successfully started a new life in a new country by opening a restaurant and serving the food of their home country.

Our desire to "sample" other cultures has also helped big brand-name food businesses to flourish. McDonald's is one of the most recognized brands in the world. The burger-and-fries food chain began life in California in 1940. Today, 47 million people in 119 countries sample a taste of "American life" every day.

▲ A McDonald's restaurant brings all-American cuisine to Tokyo, Japan.

5

▲ The process of migrant cultures integrating into a new culture, while retaining their own identity can be seen in the multitude of "ethnic" urban neighborhoods throughout Western Europe and North America. Many have names such as "Chinatown," "Little Havana," "Koreatown," or "Little Jerusalem." Here, diners in "Little Italy," New York City, enjoy Italian food and the outdoor "café culture" of the Mediterranean.

Cultural Identity: Who Am I?

Cultural identity is reflected in how a person views himself or herself and how a person views or relates to others. By identifying with a particular culture, and belonging to a group whose cultural ties are strong, a person may gain a sense of security and belonging. Feeling that people around us understand, value, and accept us gives us a sense of self-worth.

What Cultural Identity Is Based On

Cultural identity is based on a variety of factors. It may be based on race and ethnicity. It may also be based on geographical location, religion, or even one's political point of view. It is often a matter of what we "call" ourselves. We may call ourselves European, Muslim, or Liberal—or Jamaican, Hindu, or Republican. Often a single cultural identity is formed out of a mixture of cultures in the past—for example, African-American, Scotch-Irish, or French Canadian. People may identify themselves one way in certain circumstances and another way in others. For example, a tourist may call herself American while traveling abroad but refer to herself as Jewish when speaking to others in her own country.

▲ *In the area of Toronto now known as "Tehranto," shops display signs in Persian script and shopkeepers sell goods associated with the residents' home country, such as in this spice store. Persian food, such as kebab, is on sale and is almost as common in Toronto today as pizza.*

Toronto or Tehranto?

In most cases, the blending or adapting of two or more cultures occurs when one group migrates into a region inhabited by members of another culture. Usually, but not always, the migrant group reshapes itself to adapt to the dominant culture while still maintaining its own cultural identity.

One interesting version of this phenomenon exists in Toronto, Canada. Since the early 1960s, many Iranians have migrated to Canada. Most Iranian Canadians assimilated well into their multicultural setting, joining all facets of life in Canada. Still, Canadians of Iranian descent maintain a strong sense of cultural identity. As the number of Iranian immigrants grew, so did Persian businesses, particularly in the Yonge Street and Sheppard Avenue area. The area has become affectionately known among Iranian Canadians as Tehranto—a fusion of the names Toronto and Tehran—the capital city of Iran.

FOCUS ON:

HOOKAH LOUNGES

A hookah lounge is a gathering place—usually a restaurant, café, or bar—where people smoke from a large pipe known as a hookah. Most hookahs have several stems, each with a removable tip, conducting smoke that is cooled through a large water bowl. Hookahs originated centuries ago in India and are popular throughout South Asia and the Middle East, where they are often smoked in homes, tea shops, and cafés. Hookah lounges are mostly found in Western nations, particularly in cities with large Middle Eastern communities, such as Toronto and London. Hookah lounges are places where people of Middle Eastern descent can feel closer to their ancestry and connect with others of their own culture.

Hookah lounges have also sprung up in areas throughout North America and Europe with large numbers of college-age people. In North America, many cities have smoking bans, and even where bans are not in effect, many customers prefer not to smoke tobacco. Hookah lounges have adapted to the cultural mainstream, and customers may smoke non-tobacco herbs with lemon, pomegranate, and other fruit flavors. They can also enjoy tea, Turkish coffee, and Middle Eastern food.

▼ Sod houses were built by cutting out and then digging up thick, rectangular chunks of prairie grass that were used like bricks. Although the houses were well insulated and cheap to build, they could be damp and often experienced rain damage. This is a replica of a sod house in Minnesota.

Adapting to New Environments

In the natural world, all living species have adapted to the conditions in their environment as a basic means of survival. Like other mammals, humans have adapted to their environment physiologically. Features, such as body hair and skin color, vary to adapt to the environment where people have lived over many centuries.

People also adapt in other, non-biological ways. Nowhere is people's ability to change and adjust to new environments and cultural conditions more evident than in the experiences of people who have migrated and settled in North America over the last few centuries.

▶ Incoming cultures leave their mark on existing cultures. In Minnesota, which was heavily settled by Swedish and Norwegian immigrants, Scandinavian culture has infused everything from the kinds of foods Minnesotans eat to the choice of the name Vikings for the professional football team that most of them root for. Here, Ragnar, the Minnesota Vikings Mascot, spurs on the team!

Adaptation among Scandinavian Immigrants

In the 1800s, many Scandinavian families migrated to the United States from Sweden, Norway, and Denmark to take advantage of free farmland under the Homestead Act for anyone willing to work it. Once pioneers arrived at their land (usually in the Upper Midwest), they had to build homes. Though many Scandinavians were skilled carpenters, there weren't many trees on the prairies. Instead of log houses, they adapted to their new environment and built "soddys"— houses made of strips of sod, cut and stacked like bricks.

▲ *The Swedish word* smorgasbord *has worked its way into North American culture as a description of a large and generous assortment of food served buffet style. No Scandinavian celebration, such as this gathering at Christmas time, is complete without a smorgasbord, but today traditional dishes, such as* ludefisk *and Swedish meatballs, sit alongside modern recipes.*

Maintaining Traditions and Customs

Scandinavians adapted well to life in the United States, but they maintained certain customs and traditions. Nordic knitting, *hardangersøm* (a traditional type of embroidery), and *rosemaling* (Norwegian decorative painting) are some examples. Even while they maintained many of their traditional ways, Scandinavian immigrants made changes to adapt to their new surroundings. While most kept their religion, establishing Lutheran churches and schools, a few of them converted to other religions. Among them was a group of Swedes who converted to the Mormon faith.

ANGEL ISLAND

Chinese who migrated to San Francisco between 1848 and the 1900s were quarantined, questioned, and processed at an immigration processing station on Angel Island, in San Francisco Bay. They were sometimes detained for months at a time. For many, serious disappointment and culture shock set in. The walls of the immigration station on Angel Island are covered with writing. Some detainees recorded their names, events, and even poetry. Here (shown to the right) is one such poem:

國民不爲甘爲牛，
意至美洲作營謀。
洋樓高聳無緣住，
誰知棲所是監牢？

▲ *The poem translates as follows:* Instead of remaining a citizen of China; I willingly became an ox; I intended to come to America to earn a living. The Western styled buildings are lofty; but I have not the luck to live in them. How was anyone to know that my dwelling place would be prison?

Bringing China to America

Beginning in 1848, many Chinese citizens migrated to the United States. They settled in a section of San Francisco, their port of entry, about one mile (1.6 kilometers) long by 1.3 miles (two km) wide. That cramped piece of land has since become the most famous of several "Chinatowns" that have developed in other cities across North America.

Most Chinese immigrants were male. Some worked for large companies that were looking for cheap labor, and many became part of immigrant crews working on the Transcontinental Railroad, which was completed in 1869. From the earliest days of Chinese immigration to the present day, many immigrants adapted to their new home by opening laundries and other businesses that catered to their American customers.

◄ *Chinese boys (circa 1910) wait for a medical examination at the Angel Island immigration station in San Francisco Bay.*

The Value of Tradition in Times of Trouble

Chinese Americans who voluntarily migrated to America have suffered from racism, persecution, and discrimination. For decades following the first wave of Chinese immigrants in the 1800s, Chinese Americans withstood violence, bloodshed, and even laws aimed at limiting their numbers and their rights. The strength of anti-Chinese sentiment during the 1800s seems puzzling today. Back then, many U.S. citizens believed that the United States benefitted whites only. Until the arrival of Chinese immigrants, the only non-European people that most Americans had encountered were Native and African Americans. The arrival of such an exotic group was perceived by many white people as a threat to their jobs, their livelihoods, and their cultural identity as European Americans.

JOURNEY STORIES

THE JOURNEY OF LEE CHEW:

Like other Chinese immigrants of the time, Lee Chew came to North America in the late 1800s with little more than his own resources to get him through those first days.

My father gave me $100, and I went to Hong Kong with five other boys from our place and we got steerage passage on a steamer, paying $50 each. All my life I had been used to sleeping on a board bed with a wooden pillow, and I found the steamer's bunk very uncomfortable, because it was so soft. The food was different from that which I had been used to, and I did not like it at all.

I was afraid of the stews, for the thought of what they might be made of by the wicked wizards of the ship made me ill. When I got to San Francisco, . . . I was half starved, but a few days' living in the Chinese quarter made me happy again. A man got me work as a house servant in an American family, and my start was the same as that of almost all the Chinese in this country.

When I went to work for that American family I could not speak a word of English, and I did not know anything about house work. The family consisted of husband, wife, and two children. They were very good to me and paid me $3.50 a week, of which I could save $3.

▲ This woodcut illustration from 1855 shows Chinese immigrants running a laundry. Many immigrants became shopkeepers and restaurant owners.

Partly in response to this discrimination, and partly because of the strength of their own cultural ties, most Chinese Americans clung to their many traditions. One centuries-old custom that followed most Chinese immigrants to America was the shipping of the bones of a deceased person back to China for a proper burial. According to traditional belief, misfortune would befall the ancestors of those who were not properly buried in China. Today, their presence and success within the American mainstream have chipped away at the animosity that Chinese Americans endured for so long. The growth of Chinese restaurants and Chinatowns in cities all over the world is a tribute to how much Chinese culture has been embraced by mainstream cultures everywhere.

ANYONE FOR DIM SUM?

Dim Sum is a light meal of steamed dumplings and other delicacies served with traditional green tea. Dim Sum originated as a light snack served to farmers or travelers at teahouses in China. Today, it is enjoyed by people of many different cultures. In Chinese communities, Dim Sum is traditionally served in the morning through to the midafternoon. On weekends, families will often get together in a Dim Sum restaurant. Many older Chinese people like to go for Dim Sum after their morning exercise. They eat, drink tea, and read the newspapers.

Surviving a New Culture

Culture shock is a phrase that describes the negative feelings people have when they are uprooted and transplanted into a new culture. Sometimes people entering a new culture don't know what to expect of others. More importantly, they may not know what others expect of them. Feelings of anxiety and confusion mix with a dislike of certain things about the new culture. For example, foods and customs that are interesting and exciting at first can soon become annoying when the novelty wears off. This can

▲ The sport of dragon boat racing (using long, canoe-like boats decorated with a dragon's head and tail) began in China over 2,000 years ago. The races are held as part of the Duanwu Festival. Today, dragon boat racing is a popular sport worldwide. As the crew of paddlers powers the boat, a drummer provides a rhythmic beat to help crew members time their strokes.

lead to a sense of isolation. Sometimes people experiencing culture shock become depressed or even choose to return to their previous homes. Even those who do withstand culture shock don't always do so easily and it may take them a long time to adapt to their new home.

Can You Go Back Home Again?

Reverse culture shock, sometimes called re-entry shock, is what some immigrants feel when returning home. After adapting to a new culture, pace, and lifestyle, they may find it difficult to go back to the old ways. People returning to their native country may expect things to have stayed the same, but a country's culture may change over time. This makes the transition back to one's old country even more difficult. Studies of students who attend foreign universities and then return home show that they often feel sad and lonely when they realize that life has gone on without them and that friends and family don't want to hear about life abroad.

▲ *The San Francisco Police Department's dragon winds through the streets of San Francisco's Chinatown during a Chinese New Year parade. Revelers of all ages, nationalities, and cultures enjoy the annual celebration in Chinatowns around the world.*

C H A P T E R T W O
CULTURAL SUPERIORITY

Each culture is unique, but can any one culture be considered better than another? Sadly, history is full of examples of people and governments who believed their culture and civilization were not only unique but superior to others.

The Path of Cultural Intolerance

The attitude that one culture is superior to another is born of ignorance and intolerance. The results of such attitudes may be hurtful on a local or personal level. On a national or international scale, they can lead to war, religious and ethnic persecution, enslavement, and genocide, which is the deliberate killing of people, usually of different cultures or nationalities.

▲ During the time of the slave trade millions of Africans were transported on slave ships to their new "homes." Thinking only of their profits, slave traders would cram hundreds of men, women, and children onto each ship. The slaves were chained together and they had no room to move around or even stand, and no toilets. Many of the men, women, and children died during the journey.

THE LASH.

◄ "The Lash" is one of a series of artworks painted by American artist Henry Louis Stephens that show the life of a slave. Many slaves regularly received terrible beatings from their owners.

Where Do We All Come From?

Modern humans (*Homo sapiens sapiens*) originated in Africa. Around 150,000 years ago, the earliest populations of modern humans began to migrate, out of Africa. In time, their migrations took them further afield until eventually, humans had settled around the world. Given the common ancestry of the human race, it is shocking to see how cultural attitudes and beliefs have often held the idea that some people are superior to others. In more recent centuries, for example, many Europeans believed they were culturally superior to Africans and Australian Aborigines. The slave trade is a good example of how ignorance and the disregard for the value of other cultures can lead to inhumane behavior.

The Slave Trade

In 1452, Pope Nicholas V gave Afonso V of Portugal the right to make slaves out of "unbelievers" (anyone who did not hold to the beliefs of the Roman Catholic Church). This made the slave trade acceptable under Catholicism at that time and led to the kidnapping and enslavement of many Africans by the Portuguese. In time, other European nations became involved in the slave trade. It has been estimated that between the early 1500s and the early 1800s, approximately 10 million people were kidnapped and taken to the Americas to become slaves.

SLAVERY

People born into slavery in America knew no other culture than that of the Old South. Even when interviewed years after gaining their freedom, some former slaves expressed conflicting viewpoints on their life as a slave. Here, transcribed into language that reflects the original dialects, are the opinions of two former slaves.

I kin remember de days when I was one of de house servants. Dere was six of us in de ol' marster's house, me, Sarai, Lou, Hester, Jerry and Joe. Us didn't know nothin' but good times den. My job was lookin' á'ter de corner table whar nothin' but de desserts sat. My! Dem was good ol' days.

Charity Anderson, Mobile, Alabama

Slavery was the worst days was ever seed in the world. They was things past tellin', but I got the scars on my old body to show to this day. I seed worse than what happened to me... The times I hated most was pickin' cotton when the frost was on the bolls. My hands git sore and crack open and bleed.

Mary Reynolds, Dallas, Texas

The gains realized by those who engaged in the slave trade would not have been possible were it not for the sense of cultural superiority that permeated the entire business from start to finish. Africans were kidnapped from their homes, and taken away from their families. They were used as "cargo" in exchange for rum and other commodities. They were auctioned off at slave auctions like animals. Countless people in business, politics, and the military devoted their lives to maintaining or defending slavery. Every step of this process of making money from such human misery depended on people being convinced that the culture—and those who

▶ This illustration by artist Henry Louis Stephens shows African-American slaves celebrating Christmas. Music, dance, story telling, and other traditions from their homelands in West and Central Africa connected African Americans to the cultures from which they were taken. They also became the basis for a new and vibrant culture in America.

JOURNEY STORIES

HARRIET TUBMAN'S JOURNEY TO FREEDOM

Harriet Tubman was a slave who escaped from her owners in Maryland and settled in the free state of Philadelphia. Tubman would go on to help many other slaves escape to freedom. In the mid-1800s, children's writer Sarah H. Bradford published a series of interviews with Harriet Tubman:

And she started on her journey, "not knowing whither she went," except that she was going to follow the north star, till it led her to liberty. Cautiously and by night she traveled, cunningly feeling her way, and finding out who were friends; till after a long and painful journey she found, in answer to careful inquiries, that she had at last crossed that magic "line" which then separated the land of bondage from the land of freedom... "When I found I had crossed dat line," she said, "I looked at my hands to see if I was de same pusson. There was such a glory ober ebery ting; de sun came like gold through the trees, and ober the fields, and I felt like I was in Heaben." But then came the bitter drop in the cup of joy. "I had crossed the line. I was free; but there was no one to welcome me to the land of freedom. I was a stranger in a strange land; and my home, after all, was down in Maryland; because my father, my mother, my brothers, and sisters, and friends were there. But I was free, and they should be free. I would make a home in the North and bring them there, God helping me."

lived within that culture—were of such little worth that they could be easily devalued and destroyed.

Native North America

When European settlers migrated to North America in the 1500s, they brought with them their languages, customs, and religions. Indigenous people who had lived in North America for thousands of years were seen as culturally primitive—inferior to the Europeans. Centuries of conflict between the different cultures of Europe and Native America began. Native people suffered greatly from diseases brought by European settlers, removal of Native people from their lands, and outright genocide.

Native people clung to their cultural traditions, spiritual beliefs, and various forms of tribal leadership. To this day, Native people have kept their nations alive by both adapting to the ways of white America and faithfully maintaining their own cultures.

The Cherokees: From the Five Civilized Tribes ...

The Cherokees are known as one of the Five Civilized Tribes because they successfully adapted to the ways of white America. Most lived in the Southeastern United States. By the early 1800s, they had formed a government modeled in part after that of the United States and had a written constitution. In many ways, the common cultural ground between the Cherokees and European America seemed a model one.

... To the Trail of Tears

In the 1820s and 1830s, the relationship between the Cherokees and mainstream America would change forever. Most Cherokees lived in Georgia and North Carolina, but the continued migration of non-Native settlers had pushed them westward, farther and farther toward the frontier. Expanding white settlements and business interests put more pressures on the Cherokees and other Indians who were trying to keep their land—and cultures—intact.

▶ *The Cherokee published the first Native American newspaper —* The Cherokee Phoenix. *The first edition, pictured here, was printed on February 28, 1828. The newspaper is still published today.*

▲ *The Cherokee developed a writing system. This chart shows the Cherokee alphabet, or syllabary, in which each symbol represents a syllable.*

In 1830, Congress passed the Indian Removal Act. Though the Cherokees tried to fight the law in court, by 1838 they were ordered to move to Indian Territory, a region that consisted primarily of the present state of Oklahoma. An estimated 20,000 Cherokee men, women, and children were taken from their homes, herded like cattle, and forced to march over 1,000 miles (1,600 km). About 4,000 Cherokees died. The route they took as well as the journey itself became known as the *Trail of Tears*.

Australia: Another Arena for Cultural Dominance

▲ *American artist Robert Lindneux painted* The Trail of Tears *in 1942 to commemorate, or remember and honor, the suffering of the Cherokee people.*

After the American Revolution formally ended with the independence of the former British colonies in 1783, Britain set out to colonize other lands. In 1788, British ships landed at Port Jackson in Australia, claimed the country for the British Empire, and established a settlement that would become the modern-day city of Sydney. As in the Americas, Australia was already inhabited by indigenous people, known as Aborigines, who had lived in Australia for over 50,000 years.

JOURNEY STORIES

THE JOURNEY OF THE CHEROKEE

A former U.S. soldier — Private John G. Burnett — recalls his experience during the forcible removal of Cherokees to Indian Territory:

Being acquainted with many of the Indians and able to fluently speak their language, I was sent as interpreter into the Smoky Mountain Country in May, 1838... I saw the helpless Cherokees arrested and dragged from their homes, and driven at the bayonet point into the stockades. And in the chill of a drizzling rain on an October morning I saw them loaded like cattle or sheep into six hundred and forty-five wagons and started toward the west. One can never forget the sadness and solemnity of that morning. Chief John Ross led in prayer and when the bugle sounded and the wagons started rolling many of the children rose to their feet and waved their little hands good-by to their mountain homes, knowing they were leaving them forever.

▲ Legend has it that the Cherokee chiefs prayed for a sign that might give them strength. A beautiful white rose sprang from the ground wherever a woman's tears fell. To this day, the "Cherokee Rose" flourishes along the Trail of Tears.

The many different groups of Aborigines lived as hunter-gatherers in small family groups moving from place to place. An intimate understanding and appreciation of the natural world is central to Aboriginal culture. This lifestyle and culture was seen by Europeans as primitive and inferior.

An Attack on Aboriginal Culture

Once again, Europeans brought with them diseases that destroyed Aboriginal populations. Lands were taken from the Aborigines, and the new competition for food led to mass starvation. Aborigines defended themselves and their culture by attacking settlers, killing men and cattle, burning crops and homes, and driving settlers from the land that was rightfully Aboriginal. Settlers, in turn, responded to Aboriginal resistance with large-scale massacres of Aboriginal people.

Restoration and Reconciliation

By the early 1900s, many Aborigines were living impoverished lives on government-established reserves or on the fringes of cities—their traditional way of life lost and their culture eroded. Today, reconciliation between white Australians and Aborigines is an important issue. People come together at healing ceremonies and events such as concerts to remember and reconcile the past. The Australian government has worked to put right past injustices by passing legislation to restore Aboriginal land rights. Many Aboriginal communities, however, still suffer serious social problems such as poor health, unemployment, and poverty.

AUSTRALIA DAY OR SURVIVAL DAY?

Today, January 26 is a day to both celebrate and commemorate. Some people celebrate "Australia Day," while others celebrate "Survival Day."

Should the day be a celebration or a commemoration?

To many Aborigines, January 26 is a day to commemorate a deep loss—the loss of land rights and the loss of the right to practice their culture.

To many white Australians it is a day to celebrate the country's achievements past and present.

▲ Australia celebrated its bicentenary on January 26, 1988. Some celebrated the 200 years that had passed since the European "settlement" of Australia. But 40,000 people joined a march and rally in Sydney to celebrate the survival of Aboriginal culture since the "invasion" of Australia in 1788.

CHAPTER THREE

CULTURAL COERCION

The term *cultural coercion* refers to the use of force or the threat of force to get people to change their cultural values, beliefs, or expressions. This may mean using trickery or threats to prevent people from speaking their language, practicing their religion, or wearing their traditional clothing. It may also mean forcing people to swear an oath of loyalty to a set of beliefs or government that they find morally wrong.

Cultural Coercion in North America

Native Americans were not the only people in North America forced to give up their own culture or suffer terrible consequences. At least one form of cultural coercion—against Acadians in Canada—had a horrific effect on parts of what had once been French Canada. It also led to the birth of a new, vibrant, and uniquely American culture in Louisiana—the Cajun culture.

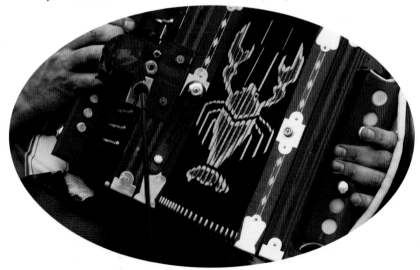

◄▲ *The predominant musical instrument in Cajun music is the fiddle. Cajun music included tunes for dancing and ballads that told stories of love, death, and Cajun history. In later years the accordion became popular in Cajun music as it could be heard easily across a crowded dance floor.*

▲ La dispersion des Acadiens *(The Dispersion of the Acadians)*, by French-Canadian artist Henri Beau, shows British soldiers forcing Acadians from their homeland.

The Acadian Expulsion

Acadia is an area that originally included the Canadian Maritime provinces, part of Quebec, and parts of what is now the Northeast United States. Today, the term Acadian refers to a French-speaking culture on the east coast of Canada.

Acadians lived under both French and British rule, forcing them to adapt culturally more than once. When Acadia transferred from French to British rule in 1710, the Acadian people had developed a strong sense of cultural identity that they were unwilling to abandon. To keep certain freedoms, they agreed to stay neutral in the event of a war between Great Britain and France.

FOCUS ON:

CAJUN CULTURE

The state of Louisiana is home to Cajun culture in North America. Cajuns are the descendants of the exiled Acadians. The word Cajun comes from an English pronunciation of the word *Acadian*. Cajuns speak a dialect of French. This and other cultural characteristics, such as their religious beliefs, folk tales, celebrations, and festivals, distinguish Cajuns as a unique ethnic group.

Cajuns are particularly known for their music and cuisine. Lively fiddle music accompanies dishes such as spicy seasoned fish and game served with rice. Cracklins are a snack made by deep-frying pork skin. Gumbo, jambalaya, and étouffe are rich dishes containing rice, meats, vegetables, and shellfish.

▲ A crawfish boil is the ultimate Cajun cook-out! Friends and family gather to boil pounds of these small lobster-like shellfish in a giant pot. Crawfish live in the mud of the freshwater bayous of Louisiana. The Cajun people settled in the bayous when they were expelled from Acadia.

▲ *A prisoner is tortured during the Spanish Inquisition. The man is tied to a revolving wheel below which a fire burns. In the background, monks wait to record the man's confession.*

This compromise was accepted for many years but when Charles Lawrence became governor of Nova Scotia in 1753, he tried to force French Acadians to swear an oath of allegiance to the British Crown. Those who stood firm in their beliefs were threatened with deportation—they would be sent away from their country. On September 5, 1755, those Acadians who had failed to satisfy the British of their loyalty were ordered to give up all their possessions to the Crown. Next, they were taken prisoner. It is estimated that approximately 14,000 Acadians were deported on ships under terrible conditions to France or other parts of North America. Thousands died of illness, drowning, starvation, and sheer misery. Surviving Acadians fled to Quebec and other French-held parts of North America, such as Louisiana, searching for a new place to call home.

The Spanish Inquisition

Persecution and torture are perhaps two of the most extreme forms of coercion. In the mid to late 1400s, a countrywide persecution of non-Catholics began in Spain. It started around 1478 and went on until about 1834. It began with the marriage of Ferdinand and Isabella, uniting the regions of Aragón and Castilla. To strengthen and unify their culturally diverse kingdom, King Ferdinand and Queen Isabella decided to force everyone to become Catholic. The main goal of the campaign that became known as the Inquisition was to convert all non-Catholic Christians to Catholicism.

One major outgrowth of the Inquisition was the targeting of non-Christians, in particular two groups that had established cultural, religious, and economic roots in Spain: Muslims and Jews. Muslims (historically known during this period as Moors) had migrated from North Africa and ruled Spain for hundreds of years. Following the expulsion of the Jews from Palestine (modern-day Israel) in the year 70, they had migrated throughout the Middle East, North Africa, and parts of Europe, particularly Spain. Muslims and Jews were forced to choose between converting to Catholicism or expulsion from Spain.

Even when people converted, the Inquisition remained obsessed with them—suspecting that they only converted to save their lives. By the time the cases of non-Catholics came to trial, their fate was probably sealed—torture and death for admitting to their "crimes," and torture and death for failing to admit to their crimes.

FOCUS ON:

METHODS OF TORTURE

The methods of torture used during times of political or religious persecution such as the Spanish Inquisition were as varied as they were barbaric. Boiling water, fire, rats, and exposure were commonly used to torture people, but much worse were the many horrifying instruments created for the sole purpose of inflicting as much pain as possible on a person. Some of these included items with names that were as colorful as they were terrifying: the thumb screw, the tongue tearer, and the head crusher.

▲ At the Museum of the Inquisition in Guanajuato, Mexico, visitors can see some of the torture implements used during the Spanish Inquisition.

CHAPTER FOUR

PRESERVATION, PROTECTION & ISOLATION

There is always a desire within any given culture to preserve and protect what makes it unique—its language, clothing, food, traditions, and religious practices and beliefs. What happens, though, when some people want to preserve their culture at the cost of other people's freedom to express theirs?

▲ *Negative feelings toward immigrants can often be used to their advantage by racist political parties. Here, members of the racist National Front political party in the United Kingdom campaign outside a mosque in London.*

▲ *In the UK the British National Party (BNP) says it exists "to secure a future for the indigenous people of these (British) islands." In 2009, with the UK economy in trouble, the BNP preyed on people's financial fears during the Euro elections by continually making a link between immigration and unemployment. The BNP received enough votes to win two seats in the European parliament. This led many people to ask: is the UK becoming a less tolerant and more xenophobic society?*

Xenophobia

Whenever a large-scale migration occurs, many people might worry about how an influx of outsiders will affect the economy and crime rate of their region. People also worry about what sort of impact the newcomers will have on their culture. This fear and suspicion can lead to a wish to protect and preserve their culture from outside influences carried in by people from another culture. These beliefs may result in an extreme form of hostility toward outsiders known as xenophobia.

The Chinese Exclusion Act

One form of xenophobia took root in the United States during the 1800s and culminated in the passage of the Chinese Exclusion Act in 1880. This was the first time that restrictions were placed on U.S. immigration. The act had several provisions to restrict or even prevent Chinese immigrants from entering the United States. One decreed that the only way a person from China could enter the country was to prove that he or she had a father who was already a U.S. citizen. Under that type of restriction, very few Chinese citizens could immigrate, and those who did make it in were not allowed to become U.S. citizens. As a result, most Chinese had virtually no contact with other Americans, preventing their assimilation into the mainstream U.S. culture until well into the 1900s.

FOCUS ON:

JOURNEY OF THE ZOROASTRIAN PARSIS

Over 1,000 years ago, a group of Parsis emigrated from their native Persia (modern-day Iran) to India. Like many migrants, they were not immediately welcomed in their new land. According to one story, the leader of the state to which they had migrated told them, "My country is overpopulated already. How would we find room for you?" In reply, the Parsi leader took a bowl, filled it to the brim with milk, and then blended a spoonful of sugar very carefully into the milk, not spilling a drop.

The Parsi leader then turned to the Indian and explained, "We are like the sugar. We will only sweeten your country."

Apartheid

The word *apartheid* literally means "apartness" or "separateness." Apartheid was the system of government in South Africa from 1948 to 1994. Under its laws, there was to be no mixing of cultures between white South Africans (descendants of the Dutch settlers who migrated to Africa in the 1600s) and native Africans. The government also separated all public services. Education and health care for white people were significantly superior to those services offered to non-whites. South Africans who opposed the system were jailed, often beaten, and even murdered. Under intense pressure from the world community and with increased resistance within in its own borders among blacks and whites alike, South Africa ended its apartheid policies in the early 1990s.

Stereotyping and Racism

An incoming migrant group may choose to protect itself rather than integrate. Negative stereotyping or racist behavior toward newcomers can further make them reluctant to socialize with other cultural groups. This form of isolation may reinforce the stereotype that immigrants are only interested in their "own kind" and not the community or the mainstream culture.

A stereotype is an oversimplified view of a group of people, usually on the grounds of race, ethnicity, or religion. Most stereotyping is negative and leads to racial prejudice and other forms of discrimination. After the terrorist attacks of September 11, 2001, members of the Muslim community (both immigrant and established) suffered from several types of stereotyping. Some people believed that many Muslims—and Arab people in particular—were terrorists, that most Muslims supported the terrorist acts, and that all Muslims were to be mistrusted or feared. Like most stereotypes, these are inaccurate, but also like most stereotypes, they are difficult to dispel.

Stereotyping, Racism, and Cultural Resistance in the United States

Groups that have been living among others for decades or even centuries may still suffer from stereotypes that date back to times when they first arrived. In the United States, for example, the most pervasive stereotypes have applied to

▲ During apartheid in South Africa people were classified as "Black," "White," "Coloured" (mixed-race), or "Asian," and they were kept separate by force.

▲ Post-9/11 stereotypes spilled over onto other cultures. Hindus, Sikhs, and people from other religious or ethnic groups found that they were thought to have terrorist ties simply because ignorant people in the larger cultural group claimed they "looked like a terrorist." Here, New York's Sikh community celebrate the Sikh New Year.

African Americans. Many of these stereotypes are linked to the attitudes of racial and cultural superiority held by Europeans and later European Americans to justify the kidnapping and enslavement of African Americans for hundreds of years.

In the years following the Civil War, many newly freed African Americans migrated to the North in search of jobs, safety, and a greater sense of security. Most black people fared better in the North than in the South, where old prejudices and resentments were still strong among white Americans and laws denying blacks voting and other rights still existed.

A New Migrant Class in the North

Life in the North has not always been easy for most African Americans. As more moved into larger northern cities, such as Detroit, Chicago, Philadelphia, and Boston, they suffered from many of the racial prejudices they faced in the South, but with an added twist—the kind of resistance faced by other migrant groups when they encounter cultures and people who resent the intrusion of newcomers. These resentments were not expressed as openly as in the South—and the laws were certainly

▲ *Like many northern cities, Boston had become heavily segregated along racial lines by the 1970s. In 1974, court-ordered busing was used as one means of desegregating Boston's schools. Opposition to busing in some of the city's predominantly white neighborhoods was so great that African-American students had to be transported back and forth under heavy police guard. In this photo, police escort buses are taking black students back to their homes in the Roxbury section from nearly all-white South Boston.*

less restrictive in the North. Nonetheless, the animosity shown to black people in previously all-white neighborhoods and schools in the North, particularly following the struggles and triumphs of the civil rights movement in the South during the 1950s and 1960s, shook the faith of many who had never imagined that race could be a "problem" in the North.

CHAPTER FIVE

INTEGRATION & ASSIMILATION

When cultures meet as a result of one group migrating and settling in an area already inhabited by other groups, some mixing of the cultures is bound to occur. What happens when people integrate into other cultures? What happens to their cultural identity—and what kind of cultural identity do their children grow up with?

◄ *In Western countries, minority cultures often stand apart from the mainstream in the types of clothing they wear. For Sikhs (top), turbans are a sign of holiness. In Orthodox Judaism, distinctive headwear (middle) is a sign of obedience to God and a way of identifying oneself as a Jew. In Islam, the hijab (bottom) is an expression of modesty and, more recently, a way of asserting one's identity as a Muslim woman.*

▲ *American fast food meets Islamic customs at Beurger King Muslim in Clichy-sous-Bois, Paris. The area has a large immigrant Muslim population from North Africa. At Beurger King Muslim customers enjoy halal burgers and chicken (meat prepared according to Islamic dietary laws) with French fries and soda.*

▲ Bahrainian sprinter Roqaya Al Ghasara (left) competes in the 200 meters at the 2008 Beijing Olympics. Al Ghasara has been eager to show the world that there is nothing constricting about wearing hijab.

The Second Generation: Children of Immigrants

The bond that first-generation immigrants have with their culture can be a source of strength and comfort as they adjust to their new surroundings. For their children, however, those cultural ties may be an obstacle to their need to become a part of the prevailing cultural landscape. First-generation immigrants usually hold tightly to their language and other cultural traditions. They may associate mainly with those of their own culture and resist assimilation.

Children born into the new environment, or introduced to it at a very young age, may reject traditional values and language and feel disconnected from their heritage—sometimes even embarrassed by it. A famous scene in the movie My Big Fat Greek Wedding has the main character eating a traditional Greek dish, mousaka, for lunch, while other children, of Anglo-Saxon descent, hurl insults. This scene, or ones like it, are not uncommon among the second-generation offspring of immigrants from other cultures. Often the flashpoint of embarrassment for kids of immigrant families is food. Sometimes it is the way their parents dress or celebrate traditional holidays. Almost always, it is language.

TRADITIONAL RELIGIOUS CLOTHING

Opinions among Muslim women differ concerning the wearing of *hijab*. The word hijab refers broadly to modest dress but is more commonly used to describe the headscarf, or headcovering, that many Muslim women wear.

Iranian writer and women's rights activist Azam Kamguian strongly opposes the veiling of women. In a speech given at rallies held in front of Iranian embassies in London, UK, and Helsinki, Finland, on *International Women's Day* 2001, Kamguian said:

... we, freedom-lovers and passionate advocates of women's rights have gathered here to protest against the mandatory veiling of women in Iran... Veiling internalises the Islamic notion in women that they belong to an inferior sex... It teaches them to limit their physical movements and their free behaviour. Veiling is a powerful tool to institutionalise women's segregation and to implement a system of sexual apartheid.

Sprinter Roqaya Al Ghasara represents her country, Bahrain, at international athletics events wearing a specially made aerodynamic veil. Al Ghasara says:

The hijab has never been a problem for me. In Bahrain you grow up with it. There are more women in sport all the time from countries like Qatar and Kuwait. You can choose to wear the hijab or not. For me it's liberating...

ARRANGED MARRIAGES

In some cultures arranged marriages are the custom. Two families will make a match between two young people—often to obtain social status or property. Around 75 percent of Indian marriages are arranged. For some young Hindus and Sikhs growing up in the UK or the United States, the idea of an arranged marriage is a tradition they are happy to embrace. For others it is an alien and unhappy prospect.

BA is against arranged marriages:

...the thought of marrying a man whom I have met twice is repulsive. Worse is the way women are "shown off" to their prospective grooms. Gone are the days when women were asked to display their teeth, but a good Indian girl must have the correct manner, culinary skills, and attributes that make her desirable in the arranged marriage market... The reason marriages like these don't break up is not because the couple is happy, but because there is huge social pressure for the marriage to work... So, you shut up and put up because you have no choice!

PB is in favor of arranged marriages:

All that's involved in a purely arranged marriage, is some sort of pre-screening process undertaken by someone other than the couple. They arrange a meeting, and then it's up to the couple to decide if they want to get married. So think about this: if you were introduced to your partner through friends or through a singles website, you've had an arranged marriage!

▲ In Western cultures people choose their own husband or wife. In traditional Indian culture a marriage arranged by your family is the norm. Many Hindu or Sikh women meet their future husband for the first time at their engagement party or, as seen here, on their wedding day.

Out with the New, In with the Old!

Sometimes the opposite occurs. In certain circumstances, parents have assimilated into the mainstream culture, downplayed their own culture to avoid "trouble" or embarrassment for themselves or their families, or even embraced the mainstream culture with open arms. The effect of this large-scale effort to "fit in" may be a rejection of their cultural roots. Likewise, in some instances, the second-generation children of such parents may seek out on their own a strong return to their cultural roots. In some cases, they may even return to their parents' country of origin to visit or settle. In other cases, they may decide to learn the language and dress in traditional clothing.

Spanish, Univision, and Telemundo

The United States has large Spanish-speaking communities, most of them the result of migrations of people from Mexico, Puerto Rico, Cuba, and other parts of Latin America and the Caribbean. Some of these communities have their roots in parts of the United States, such as

California, New Mexico, and Colorado, that once belonged to Mexico. In these communities, the roots of Latino culture may be just as strong as those of the mainstream Anglo culture.

Spanish has become the most widely spoken non-English language in America because of the size and widespread numbers of Latinos in the United States. With the widespread use of Spanish has come a variety of ways in which it has worked itself into—or at least alongside —mainstream American culture. Two television networks based in the United States—Univision and Telemundo—have made Spanish-language TV a regular part of the lives of Hispanic Americans. They have also exposed non-Hispanic Americans both to the Spanish language and to Latino culture. One of the networks—Telemundo—now offers programming in Spanglish—a mixture of English and Spanish that produced a uniquely "American" form of Spanish. Telemundo has also added English subtitles to some programs in order to attract second-generation Hispanics who may not speak Spanish.

▲ One staple of the Telemundo schedule are telenovelas — soap opera-style miniseries. Telenovelas generally run for about 120 episodes, airing five or six times per week. The popular ABC comedy Ugly Betty starring America Ferrera began life as a telenovela called Yo soy Betty, la fea (I'm Betty, the ugly one) on Colombian TV in 1999.

FOCUS ON:

GOT SPANGLISH?

Spanglish is a hybrid version of Spanish and English. Many of the words are rooted in English with Spanish constructions built out of them. Others are words that already have other meanings in Spanish but are so similar to English words that they now have the English meaning applied to them. In the list of Spanglish words that follows, non-Spanish speakers may recognize some terms as sounding "made up," having an almost comic effect. This impression isn't entirely wrong, as Spanglish is a way of speaking that can easily take on new words and expressions as quickly as people come up with them. Here are a few examples:

- averaje (a-ve-RAH-je) — *average*
- boila (BOY-lah) — *heating appliance, boiler*
- brecas (BRAY-kas) — *breaks*
- carpeta (kar-PE-tah) — *carpet*
- chopin (TCHO-peen) —
  1. *Shopping center mall*
  2. *Going shopping*
- deiof (dey-OF) — *day off*
- frizer (FREE-zer) — *refrigerator*
- grocear (gro-SEAR) — *to acquire groceries*
- jonrón (khon-RON) — *home run*
- lonche (LONCHE) —
  1. *Midday meal*
  2. *Food served to guests at an event*
- marqueta (mar-ke-tah) — *supermarket*

CHAPTER SIX

FUSION

Many people believe that in order to survive, cultures must be free to adapt and change with the times. The "swapping" of cultures—whether in areas of food, art, music, language, or any avenue of everyday life— is enriching and encourages tolerance and cooperation, because each culture is giving as well as taking.

Two Great Multicultural Cities

New York City, in the United States, and London, in the United Kingdom, are examples of cities that have successfully grown in size and diversity. Each city has become a model of cultures that have fused with one another and the mainstream, and have maintained the unique identity they carried with them into the mix.

▲ Ellis Island (foreground) sits at the mouth of the Hudson River in New York Harbor. It was the point of entry to the United States for more than 12 million immigrants. Today, the immigration station building is home to a museum telling the tale of those immigrants, whose descendants make up almost half the population of Americans today.

◀ Top to bottom: Entertainers Adam Sandler, Sarah Michelle Gellar, Julia Louis-Dreyfus, and Jerry Seinfeld all have roots in New York City's immigrant Jewish community.

▲ *A world of celebrations in New York, clockwise from upper left: The Macy's Thanksgiving Day parade; a marching band in the St. Patrick's Day parade; revelers at the annual Brazilian Day Festival in Little Brazil; the Hindu spring festival of Holi celebrated in Queens.*

New York City

Many people consider New York to be the cultural capital of the United States. It has numerous museums, art galleries, and theaters. It is the city that gave birth to modern dance and the comic book. It is the subject and setting of many movies and television programs.

New York has been shaped over hundreds of years by cultures that have come from other lands. It is one of the most culturally diverse cities in the world, with distinct communities of Puerto Ricans, Chinese, Dominicans, Jamaicans, Russians, Italians, Jews, Poles, East Indians, Greeks, Egyptians, Albanians, Colombians, and countless others. Manhattan boasts neighborhoods with names like Chinatown, Little Italy, and Spanish Harlem. The city also has a higher Jewish population than any city in Israel, and more Jews than any country in the world outside of Israel.

You can get just about any kind of food in the world in New York's many restaurants and grocery stores. People in the city celebrate every religious and national holiday imaginable, and the various parades and festivals reflect its incredible diversity of cultures.

LONDON

Like New York, London is an enormous international center brimming with cultural diversity. Over 300 distinct national and ethnic groups can be counted among approximately 13 million residents. With over 300 different languages spoken, London is considered the most linguistically diverse city in the world. Museums, art galleries, theaters, and cinemas offer a wide variety of cultural experiences, and food is as diverse as it is tasty.

▲ *Many West Indians from the Caribbean settled in the Notting Hill area of London. In 1964 they started the annual Notting Hill Carnival, a celebration of music and dance with extravagant costumes, floats, and the music of the Caribbean — calypso, reggae, and steel bands.*

Migration and the Arts: African-American Influences on Music

The forced migration of Africans during the slave trade had a profound effect on American culture. Everything from food to language to fashion to the arts was dramatically affected by a people whose roots grew deep and stretched across two continents. One aspect of African-American culture that changed not only America, but much of the world, was music.

The Blues, R & B, and More

The expressive musical style known as the blues was born of church hymns, ballads, and rhythmic dance tunes. It originated in the late 1800s and early 1900s in the South and moved into the North and Midwest as African Americans migrated northward. Its soulful style is characterized by the performer singing a line and having his or her instrument perform a type of response.

▲ *Clockwise, from upper left: James Brown, Ray Charles, B.B. King, and Louis Jordan (playing the saxophone). Each of these legendary African-American performers embodies the fusion of soul, R & B, the blues, jazz, and rock 'n' roll into a uniquely American musical tradition.*

▲ *Latin dances such as the tango, cha-cha, and mambo grew in popularity in the United States along with the number of immigrants from places such as Cuba, Puerto Rico, Colombia, and the Dominican Republic. Though many forms of Latin dance are popular, none surpasses the salsa. The term salsa was created in New York, though the dance itself is a fusion of various Latin and Afro-Caribbean dances.*

34

As African Americans moved around more, their music spread as well. Most of that music has become an essential thread in the fabric of popular American music. It includes rhythm and blues, or R&B, which in the 1940s and 1950s became one of the most recent ancestors of rock 'n' roll. Out of R & B, a host of other threads have emerged, including soul, funk, disco, and Hip-Hop.

▲ *Shown here performing in 2009, Rapper KRS-One has been a pioneer in Hip-Hop music and culture since the release of his first album in 1987. Born to Jamaican parents in New York City in 1965, he has been credited with bringing elements of Jamaican music into American Hip-Hop.*

Hip-Hop

Hip-Hop music sprang from the African-American and Latino street cultures of New York. It has a rich past, with roots in various other R & B styles, many dating back to the 1950s. It further evolved with 1970s New York DJs "sampling" bits of popular music and working them into their own lyrical and rhythmic stylings. More recently, Hip-Hop has exploded into a worldwide cultural phenomenon.

FOCUS ON:

MOTOWN— WHERE SOUL GLIDES INTO POP

In 1959, former boxer and autoworker Berry Gordy hung a sign that read "Hitsville, U.S.A." above the windows at 2648 W. Grand Blvd. in Detroit, Michigan. Motown Records was born. In just a few years, this business, which began during the peak of the civil rights movement, would reshape the entire music industry. It was a black-owned-and-operated business with its roots in African-American soul. It had a style and beat to it that drew in both black kids and white kids who by the early 1960s were into their own love affair with rock 'n' roll. Artists such as Smokey Robinson and the Miracles, the Temptations, the Supremes, the Four Tops, Marvin Gaye, the Jackson 5, and Stevie Wonder all recorded their songs under the Motown label. These artists, in turn, influenced artists of other cultures, ultimately shaping pop music around the world.

▲ This painting created in the 1870s shows British officials and their Indian servants relaxing on a shady veranda watching an elephant duel.

Where We Live and How We Speak

Language is not just a collection of sounds that communicate meaning. Language is constantly growing, changing, and adapting itself to new environments and uses. It's no big surprise, then, that when cultures come into contact with one another and ideas are swapped, so are words.

But I Thought I Was Speaking English!

In many parts of the world, the very fact of people migrating from one nation to another is enough to create a "swap" of cultural attributes, including language. During the 1700s and 1800s, for example, when British colonizers migrated to South Asia (which includes present-day India, Pakistan, Bangladesh, and Sri Lanka), new concepts and new words entered the English language. Here are a few examples:

Bungalow—a roofed porch; from a Hindi word for "house in Bengal style"

Curry—a spicy dish served in a sauce with spicy ingredients; from a Tamil word for "sauce"

Pajamas—loose pants or shirt worn for sleeping; from a Persian word for "leg garment"

Thug—a tough or violent person; from a Hindi word for "thief"

Veranda—a covered porch; from a Hindi word for "roofed open area attached to a building"

▲ *The term "bling" originated in Hip-Hop culture. Here, American rapper Paul Wall shows off his diamond-encrusted grill or teeth. Wall designs grills for top rap stars and is a partner in "TV Jewelry"—a store specializing in grills and bling jewelry.*

Urban Slang

For years, migrations have brought members of many ethnic cultures into cities and towns throughout North America. These migrations have spread the food, music, and language of these cultures beyond their origins. Today, the age of electronic communication has brought a new dimension—and a host of new media—to the swapping of words, phrases, and popular expressions. Television, movies, and digital technology—the Internet in particular—have had a tremendous impact on the speed and quantity of information, including new ways of speaking, that we now swap with the click of a button or a mouse.

With the explosion of street culture such as rap and Hip-Hop, new fashions and new varieties of English have emerged. Many of the terms in what some call urban slang have become fused with the mainstream culture. Here are just a few words and expressions that have recently had their moments of fame and, quite possibly by the time you read this book, dropped out of fashion:

Bling—flashy jewelry; relating to the effect of light reflecting off of shiny objects

Five-0—the police; derived from the name of the fictional Hawaii state police force used as the title of the popular American TV series *Hawaii Five-O*

Foshizzle (sometimes *fashizzle*)—meaning "fo' sure" or "for real" (originated by rapper Snoop Dogg)

4-1-1—information on a person or event; derived from *411*, the number used for telephone directory assistance in the United States and Canada

▲ *Today, new words can come into use and be spread around the world fast by TV, the Internet, and text messaging.*

British India— Centuries of Cultural Encounters

For centuries, all or part of India was under the domination of the British East India Company or the government of Britain. When India achieved its independence from the United Kingdom in 1947, the country was partitioned, or broken up, into two nations—India (which was mostly Hindu) and Pakistan (which was mostly Muslim). Mass migrations took place at the time, with many Muslims leaving India for Pakistan and Pakistani Hindus fleeing to India.

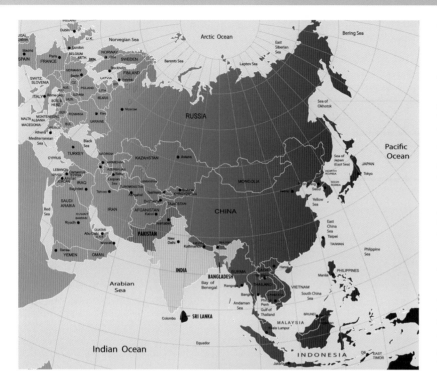

▲ *This map of South Asia shows the nations that formerly made up India when it was under British rule. When the British left in 1947, Pakistan (orange) was partitioned off as an independent nation. In 1971, the nation of Bangladesh (green) was created out of what had formerly been East Pakistan.*

▶ *Thousands of Indian cricket fans welcome back their team after they beat Pakistan in the Twenty20 World Cup in South Africa in 2007. Years of political strife and war between India and Pakistan have led to one of the most fervent sports rivalries in the world. A cricket match between the two countries can attract up to 100 million passionate TV viewers!*

◄ *India (in blue) competes against Pakistan during an ICC Champions Trophy cricket match at Edgbaston, Birmingham, UK, in 2004.*

Since the creation of the independent nations of India and Pakistan, the two countries have been at war at least four times, mostly over disputed land. In 1971, during one of those wars, East Pakistan, which was separated from West Pakistan by about 1,000 miles (1,600 km) of Indian territory, achieved its own independence and became the nation of Bangladesh.

When the British established themselves in India, they brought with them their customs, traditions, form of government, and sports. Some aspects of British culture, including the English language and the British system of government, became fused with Indian culture. When they left, the British left a country and its many cultures with little to unite them and many centuries-old hostilities to divide them. One remnant of British culture that was left behind, however, had come to be so strongly rooted in the culture of India that it has united all three nations—India, Pakistan, and Bangladesh—in a common goal. That goal: to beat one another at cricket.

CRICKET—A LASTING LEGACY OF BRITISH INDIA

Cricket, a sport using a bat and ball, dates back to the 1500s. By the mid-1800s, it had become popular enough in British India that it was no longer being played solely by British colonialists. Though it is not the official sport of India and the other South Asian nations that had once been part of India (Pakistan and Bangladesh) or that had been under British rule (the island nation of Sri Lanka), it is certainly the most popular.

In turn, South Asians who have migrated to North America have brought their love of cricket with them. Cricket was possibly the most popular sport in Canada until the early 1900s when ice hockey began its run to become Canada's most popular sport. In more recent decades, cricket suffered a further loss of interest with the introduction of big-league baseball and basketball. In recent years, with the migration of many South Asians to cities like Toronto, cricket is seeing a comeback in Canada.

Architecture

From the magnificent pyramids of ancient Egypt to the incredible temples, pyramids, and palaces of the Aztecs, Mayans, and other great indigenous civilizations of Mexico and Central America, architecture has always represented a people's culture and environment. Just like language and fashion, architecture is affected by culture and human migration.

Moorish Architecture

In the year 711, soldiers crossed over from North Africa to the Iberian Peninsula (home to present-day Spain and Portugal). There, they began a conquest and occupation of most of the peninsula that would last for nearly 800 years. The conquerors and those who migrated in their footsteps, called Moors and similar ethnically to the Arabs and other inhabitants of present-day North Africa, were primarily Muslim, although Jews living in North Africa under Muslim rule also settled in Iberia. Under Islamic rule, many Iberians converted to Islam, so that by the year 1200, almost six million of the seven million residents of the peninsula—most of them native inhabitants—were Muslim.

▲▼ *Here, we see Muslim inscriptions and a courtyard at the Alhambra Palace in Granada, Spain. Built in the mid-1300s, Alhambra was the palace and fortress of the Moorish leaders of the region. Below, archways inside the Great Mosque at Córdoba, Spain.*

The migration and rule of the Moors had a huge impact on the architecture of Spain. Although Spain is no longer a Muslim country, Islamic-style buildings can be appreciated today, especially in the southern part of the country, where Muslim culture flourished the longest. Two of the most famous examples of Moorish architecture are the Great Mosque at Córdoba and the Alhambra at Granada. Built in the 1300s, the Alhambra is the only medieval Islamic palace to survive mostly intact.

◄ *Islamic culture influenced Spain's architecture for many centuries. Islamic architectural features such as archways, detailed carvings with natural motifs, mosaic tiles, and tranquil, shady courtyards are still used in Spain's buildings today.*

What's for Dinner?

"I really have a craving for enchiladas. How about some Mexican?"

"I feel like some sweet-and-sour chicken. Let's have Chinese."

"I could use a curry. Can we have Indian?"

"I'd love a plate of lasagna. Can we eat Italian?"

"A plate of hummus with olive oil and pita! Let's do Middle Eastern."

Chinese. Mexican. Indian. Italian. Middle Eastern. These are all terms that have become familiar to North Americans looking for something a little more "fun" in a meal. In fact, some of these terms are so familiar that we hardly think of them as having origins with cultures from other parts of the world.

▲ *Along with music and language, the food we eat is one of the more exciting and entertaining ways that migration fuses different cultures.*

▲ The first known recipe for pasta made with tomato sauce was written in 1839 by Ippolito Cavalcanti, Duke of Buonvicino. Buonvicino is a town in what is today southern Italy.

▲ Diners enjoy Chinese food at a restaurant in Chinatown, New York City, in 1905.

▲ Eating "Chinese" today caters to people who enjoy combining the novelty of chopsticks with the speed, convenience, and on-the-go portability of cardboard containers.

Spaghetti

So you thought spaghetti was about as Italian as you can get? Well, it's not. Archaeologists have found evidence that noodles were being made in China around 4,000 years ago. The Jerusalem Talmud, also called the Palestinian Talmud or the Talmud of the Land of Israel, a book written between the years 220 and 375, refers to dried noodles that were bought from a vendor and boiled. When Arab people from this region conquered the large island off the "toe" of Italy known today as Sicily, they most likely brought with them this portable type of noodle and introduced it to locals in Sicily. So when did pasta meet tomato? Well, again, we look to migration. When the Spanish returned from their explorations of the Americas during the 1500s, they brought with them, among other things, a strange fruit they named the golden apple—the tomato!

Chinese Food

In the 1800s, when many Chinese migrated to America, they brought with them a style of cooking unknown to Americans. In order to cater to their non-Chinese customers, Chinese restaurant owners began to use local ingredients and to adapt to the local tastes. The result was the creation of new dishes—so-called Chinese food—that was neither found in China nor eaten by Chinese people. This type of food, sometimes referred to as either American or

Canadian Chinese cuisine, until recently was what most North Americans had in mind whenever they clamored for "Chinese." In more recent years, restaurants have appeared that feature more traditional Chinese foods. These restaurants serve food from a variety of regions in China, with a greater emphasis on vegetarian dishes, less deep frying, and in general food that is fried quickly and without animal fat.

Citizens of a Multicultural World

Today, many of us live in communities that are a mix of many different cultures due to centuries of migration and settlement. Sadly, some people still cling to the idea that the only worthwhile culture is their own. Happily, however, most of us celebrate our own origins and culture while respecting those of our neighbors. We also enjoy the many benefits—food, music, and celebrations—of living in a multicultural world.

FOCUS ON:

CARIBANA!

Many people have migrated to Canada and the United States from the Caribbean islands of Jamaica, Barbados, Haiti, and Trinidad and Tobago.

Caribana—a celebration of Caribbean culture held in Toronto every summer around the first weekend in August—attracts more than one million participants in what has been billed as North America's largest street festival. The event began in 1967 as the Caribbean contribution to Canada's centennial celebration and has continued since. The two-week celebration is a summertime version of the Carnival and Mardi Gras festivals held in many places earlier in the year to mark the beginning of the season leading up to Easter. Caribana brings together a wide range of music, dances, and foods. There are many exciting events, including calypso music shows; dances called *jump-ups*; parties called *fêtes*; masquerade, or *mas*, competitions; steel drum street parties called *pan blockos*; and story tellers and comedians performing in talk tents. The festival ends with a huge picnic.

◄ *Elaborate and fantastical costumes are an important part of the festival parade during Caribana in Toronto, Canada.*

GLOSSARY

abolition The act of completely eliminating, destroying, or revoking a law or practice; often used to describe the elimination of slavery

Anglo English or pertaining to the people or culture of England; often used to distinguish people who speak English as their native tongue from those who speak Spanish or who are of Hispanic descent in the United States

assimilation The process of one cultural group absorbing or integrating characteristics of another

centenary Relating to or consisting of a 100th anniversary or celebration

civil rights movement A movement in the United States, usually thought of as beginning in the 1950s and culminating in the passage of legislation in the 1960s, whose aim was to abolish laws and actions that discriminated against African Americans and deprived them of the same rights as other Americans

colonize To migrate to and establish a settlement in a place somewhere other than in one's own country

culture shock Feelings of anxiety and confusion experienced after being transplanted into a new cultural environment

dialect A subdivision of a language spoken in a specific area with local characteristics and peculiarities

environment The area in which something exists or lives

exotic Something new or different, usually due to its having been introduced from a foreign country

Hispanic Relating to or derived from the culture of Spain; a person in the United States who has Spanish ancestry

indigenous Native to or originating from a particular place, usually at or near where it is found

infrastructure The basic system of organization or structures, such as utilities, roads, or buildings, required for the operation of a society

intolerance The refusal to allow others to have their opinions, to follow their chosen religion, or to live in the way they choose or in a way traditional to their culture

Latino Of or relating to Latin American cultures or languages in the United States; usually in relation to people of Hispanic ancestry, but may include other languages and cultures associated with Mexico, the Caribbean, or Central and South America

Moors A historical term referring to the people of North Africa, usually Muslim, who conquered Spain in the 700s. Today, some consider this a negative or derogatory term

novelty Something that is refreshingly or surprisingly new or unusual

persecution The inflicting of pain, suffering, or harm on someone, especially for reasons of racial, religious, or ethnic background

physiologically Relating to the form and function of living things

racism Discriminatory or abusive behavior toward those of a specific race

reconciliation The settling and resolution of differences and arguments and the restoration of harmony and friendship

Scandinavians People from Norway, Sweden, and Denmark (and sometimes Iceland or Finland)

segregation A social system that provides separate facilities for minority groups

steerage The cheapest accommodations on a ship

stereotyping Representing a group of people by a widely held but oversimplified set of characteristics or images, usually based on race, ethnicity, or religion

Talmud The body of Jewish law and legend. There are two volumes of the Talmud—the Palestinian or Jerusalem Talmud and the Babylonian Talmud

xenophobia An irrational fear of foreigners or strangers

IDEAS FOR DISCUSSION

- What cultures have influenced your city, town, or country? Name some of the characteristics of those cultures and describe how they affect your life.

- Trace your ancestry as far back as you can. Did you or any of your ancestors migrate from another country? If so, what was the reason?

- Describe what aspects of your ancestry or culture you may have felt you have had to hide or play down. What were they, what were the reasons for hiding them, and how did it make you feel to do this?

- Describe what you think the term "pop culture" means. In what ways has pop culture influenced the clothing, language, and musical tastes of you and others of your age?

- Do you think it is important for cultures to adapt or should they try and remain "pure"? Explain why you feel the way you do.

FURTHER INFORMATION

http://xroads.virginia.edu/~hyper/wpa/wpahome.html
Listen to the voices of American slavery as captured during interviews with over 2,300 former slaves, most of them born around or during the time of the Civil War (mid-1800s), conducted during the 1930s.

www.eyewitnesstohistory.com/eyindx.htm
Read hundreds of firsthand accounts of historical events, many dealing with migration, on this easy-to-navigate Web site.

www.nps.gov/elis/index.htm
http://angelisland.org/immigr02.html
Ellis Island, in New York Harbor, was long the main entryway on the East Coast for people immigrating to the United States. Angel Island, located in San Francisco Bay, was once home to the Immigration Station that served as the West Coast entrance for many immigrants. See amazing photos of both of these historic sites and read more about what it was like for immigrants passing through them.

www.everyculture.com/index.html
Learn about numerous cultures of the world through this cultural encyclopedia.

www.buzzle.com/articles/world-cultures-heritage/
Read articles, stories, and accounts of hundreds of events and phenomena in world culture and heritage on this remarkable Web site.

INDEX

INDEX

ABOUT THE AUTHOR

Marina Cohen has a Master's Degree in French Literature from the University of Toronto and has been teaching since 1995. She has two middle-grade fantasy novels published (Shadow of the Moon, Trick of the Light) and one Young Adult novel (Ghost Ride). In addition to this book, her nonfiction credits include two books in the Let's Relate to Genetics series, two books in the Crabtree Character Sketches series and one book in the My Path to Math series — all published by Crabtree.

JUN - - 2010